Have Knife, Will Travel

Have Knife, Will Travel

Poems from a surgeon
on cancer, cake and crossing continents

Satya Bhattacharya

PREFACE

There are some things I should say at the outset. I grew up in Bombay (Mumbai) and now live in London. Moving from one country to another, building a career there, and defining yourself in the process, is a complicated journey. That is inevitably reflected in what I write. Also, I am a surgeon. I fix the inner plumbing of fellow humans. I have spent much of my working life in London, in the city's poorer but perhaps more interesting boroughs, operating on people's bellies. That work seeps into my poems too. This is my first collection of poems. I see them as my relatively uncomplicated responses to the people and the world around me. I hope you will find some familiar strands. Some poems are about matters political, and I do not expect you to agree with everything that I say.

While I still have a day job, all profit from this book in the UK will go to the charitable enterprises of a hospital I work in, The London Clinic. Profit made overseas will go to a charity in India run by alumni of my medical school.

I am grateful to my wife and daughter, who have given me the time to write and been my first sounding boards. I am thankful to friends who have taken time to read these poems and given me encouragement and useful feedback. I could not have done without the help from the team at SpiffingCovers, particularly with the editing, typesetting and the design for the cover. Charles Sweeney has very kindly designed the website for the book.

Satya Bhattacharya

July 2021, London

To

The patient one

CONTENTS

Rainy day

It is one of those days when the sky is grey
The rain fills the gutters with leaves
The earth turns into mushy clay
The birds quietly hunker in the eaves

No sounds but the endless drumming of raindrops
Or is it the roof leaking again?
All energy is gone, all work stops
The mind retreats into a sleepy terrain.

As a child this would be a wonderful day
When I would curl up with a book
Get cosy under a fat blanket
In my favourite nook

But the book would often soon give way
To my private fantasy
I would ride in armour, out to battle
And the princess would be in love with me.

Well the nook and the blanket are still there
And the rain isn't going away
But the princess is about to look in on me
And ask why I am wasting my day.

Doors

What do you do with a door
But go through it?
The trouble is most don't have a sign
Like "Lion enclosure"
That tells you to beware!
They just turn up
And more often than not
You just walk through
And you find what you find.

But doors are important too.
Whenever you have spent
Long enough in a room
And the air gets stifling
It is important to find a door
And open it. Soon.

Many of those I admire
Have had a knack for this
They have known when to shut
A door behind them
And when to open another.

Reflecting on necks, while digging the garden

The deep orange of the robin's breast as it plays hide-and-seek
The narrow neck of the lily where the hummingbird dips its beak
The black band round the neck of the green parakeet
The neck of the pitcher plant where the ant loses its feet
The slender throat of the heron down which the fish finally slips
The hollow in your neck where my mouth rests before it seeks your
lips

England

You think you know
Exactly what you are doing.
It's going to be a fling,
A brief affair.
She's pretty enough,
But there's so much about her
That you don't like.
And then suddenly...
You're hooked.
Committed.
Came here for five years.
This year
Will be twenty-five.

A toast

I worry for you my friend —
Neither you nor I know
If that shadow on your scan
Will shrink or continue to grow.

Life – alas — has pitched us
Thousands of miles apart.
While on the phone, we bravely smile
But worry gently gnaws at my heart.

Let me, now, as dusk
Draws in by stealth,
Look at the evening sun on the wings of a gull
And raise a toast to your health.

Mare Nostrum

A young man is floating in the water.
Through the puffiness
Of death, and the mottling
And the snot trickling out
Of his nostrils,
You can see he was handsome.
Probably twenty or twenty-two.
Sharp nose, deep-set eyes,
Now closed,
Features that suggest he was Algerian perhaps,
Or Libyan, or Tunisian.
Frayed jeans, a padded jacket
A couple of sizes too large.

The water is shallow.
You can see the shingle three feet below.
He has reached his destination
But not the way he would have wished.

I wonder where he came from.
May be a mountain village
Where the olive trees are soaking up
The sunshine, and his mother,
Perhaps sweeping the yard, is
Squinting up at the sun and
Wondering where
Her son is.

What is he doing?
Has he eaten?
His last phone call was four days ago.

Maybe there is a girlfriend too.
Combing her hair,
Looking into the mirror,
And thinking of him
As she pulls out the drawer
Where she keeps her trinkets
And looks at the photo she
Keeps hidden.

What brought him here?
What might he have said
If I ever met him?

Little swarms of tiny fish
Nibble away at his feet.
We live and die by our decisions
You say, and
He obviously made one that
Went horribly wrong.
Not your fault
Nor mine.
Yet, if I were in his shoes
The fish would be
Nibbling at mine.

Advice to a nephew starting medical school

The curriculum is devised
By unimaginative tutors
For incurious students.
Be inquisitive.

Echoes

Caught up in the moment
You do not realise, how
It will ricochet through your life

The look of invitation
The seemingly nonchalant touch
The nod of acquiescence

What you did not say
What you should have done
How the sunlight fell that day

Little do you know, how
This will all
Ricochet through your life

Good morning Mrs Giraffe

Every day I drive past the giraffe's house
At the zoo.
Most mornings she is standing at the window
Looking out.
I wave at her as I go by.
And she nods at me,
I think.
I like the sign she has put out recently
Saying she loves the NHS.

End of days

The woods are silent
Fish don't run the rivers any more
Locusts and smoke fill the air
Glaciers melt
Bush fires burn and burn

City dwellers choke on smog
But it's viruses we wear masks for
Stowaways die in freezing trucks
Children sit in cages
While we build walls taller and longer

All mirrors are banned near the naked emperor
Tyrants and fools are centre stage
Trolls rant and shout
Wise men learn to keep their counsel
So they don't have their tongues cut out

History tells us, if we care to listen,
This is how civilisations end
Have ended over centuries past
We weren't the first
We won't be the last

The time has come, friends, for last orders
For the final songs to be sung
Look around you
And tell me honestly
This isn't our Götterdämmerung

Newham Hospital

They say it was built on a rubbish dump
Out here on the distant perimeter
Of town, where the houses fade away
And factories and marshes
Stretch down to the river.

It's been here for years now.
Typical low-slung hospital architecture
From the eighties.
Faded, worn walls
Multilingual signs
Long corridors, with the usual number
Of lost bumbling souls
And among them, familiar faces
Who smile at me.

It has been busy over the years
Trainee surgeons used to call it 'Nam.
It serves a hard-bitten neighbourhood
That earns new adjectives at every census
Most diverse, most deprived...

But these last years
Have just seen gentle decline.
Like when they moved my office
To a Portakabin for good.

There's a flower bed
And a patch of lawn
Out towards the front
Where the cars pull in
And every day the diligent gardener
Picks out the cigarette butts
From the shrubs that stand.

There was an enlightened
Estates manager once
Who created a Zen garden
And a little pond
In a tiny square between two wards.
A brief valiant effort
Lent cadence by a mother duck
Who turned up several summers in a row
To rear her babies in that tiny pond.

She doesn't come any more.
The garden is overgrown.
I am still here though
Over twenty-five years now
Still seeing my daily flock
Of the infirm and the ill.
Still smiling back.

Flies

On the windowsill of my bedroom in the holiday cottage
Lie nine dead flies.
How did they get here?
Did they all fly in together
In a spirit of exploration through an open door?
Was this their K2 expedition gone all wrong?
Or did they come in one by one?
Why then did they all converge on this window?
The other windows bear no corpses!
Or... were they born in here?
I envision something rotting,
Crawling with maggots.
It all smells clean though
Of lavender air freshener.
I get a brush and dustpan
Scoop them up and throw them out of the window.
Dead, they finally achieve what
They died trying to do.

Dassera

Every breath is laboured
A faint sweat on your brow
Stubble on your cheeks
Eyes closed
No response to any stimulus.

I sit beside your bed
Waiting.

There is nothing else to be done.

Outside the drums beat.
The goddess is leaving.

Marylebone High Street

Expensive you say, that T-shirt?
Purchased from an overpriced shop.
Probably made by Third World kids
Living on gruel and slop.
Well, don't wear it, my darling,
If it makes you feel troubled
Put it aside for another day
When you reasoning is less garbled

The NHS is overly reliant on foreigners, she said

Should I be here, you ask?
A home-grown surgeon would have done this job
Equally well. Perhaps better.
Of course, but was there one?

I trained in another corner of the planet
So you got me for free.
Thirty years a surgeon
Ten thousand operations
Three hundred juniors trained
And now you have a problem with me?

Fine, look me in the eye
And say directly to me that
I have brought nothing of value.

To all bakers

Here are some useful tips
For all fellow bakers,
I don't mean the bread-wallahs
But the sponge-cake-makers.

All cakes have four ingredients
That ultimately matter –
Sugar, eggs, butter and flour
All go into your batter.

The amount of butter that goes into a cake
Is not a matter for mirth!
The more you add, the more you find
It enhances your girth.

I have found by trial and error
– You could call it a creative spurt –
That you can halve the butter in your cake
And replace it with yogurt.

Take half the weight of butter
That your recipe doth recommend
Soften it, or melt it (gently in a microwave?)
And in a bowl, with the sugar blend.

Then add an equal amount
Of zero or low-fat yogurt
Mix that well with the sugar and butter
There, that's not too much effort!

As for the sugar too,
I generally find,
If you use two thirds of what the recipe says
Your taste buds will not mind.

When it comes to eggs I can usually do
With two when the recipe says four,
But I haven't tried aquafaba for eggs
As suggested in folklore.

Finally, when it comes to flour
I have another fake:
Replace half the flour with ground almonds
To get a crumblier bake.

Or, rather than ground almonds,
Semolina you could choose.
If you're anti-gluten, instead of flour,
Cornmeal you can use.

Switching half the butter for yogurt
Makes for a moister cake.
Remember when you set the timer
A bit longer you may have to bake.

There you go, I hope you like
These modest baking tips.
Anything that keeps our cakes
From going to our hips!

Young

We were young once
You and I
Green saplings for limbs
Hearts that pumped effortlessly
Minds alert
Eyes keen
We had worlds to conquer
We would be rich
We would be famous

Your clothes would fall in a bunch
Around your feet
As you rushed into my arms.

It is quieter now.
Physical challenges measured in aliquots
No mad escapades
Or crazy parties
I tuck you into bed
As I put my book aside
And prepare to turn the light off.

Petrichor

Handling loam
Strokes some primordial tendrils
At the back of my mind.

This smell of soil, of worms.

The feel on my fingers
Of lumpy earth, pebbles,
Grit getting beneath
My fingernails –

As if I have done
This all my life.

It perhaps awakens
Memories that belong
To the species, rather
Than the individual.

It was always thus
For my ancestors –
Squatting by the field,
Looking at the sky,
Gauging the sun, the clouds,
Sniffing the air for a hint of rain
Watching the crops day
By day, as they grew.
The soil was your life.
And yours in death.
It is an umbilical smell
This fragrance of damp earth.

23rd June 2016

You came into the kitchen,
As I sat eating breakfast.
"Who are you?" you asked
"And what are you doing in my house?"

"Hey!" I replied
"I have been here
For twenty years,
Looking after you,
Cooking your food,
Cleaning the house,
Babysitting your children,
Caring for you when you have been ill.
What do you mean, who am I?"

"No," you said,
"I do not know you.
And now will you please
Leave."

Fez

The gentle, winter sun will be
Shining now in Fez
On the flat rooftops.
The bowls will be full
Of oranges.
Why are you and I not there?

Scalpel song

Give me your bodies.
Come to me with
Your sores, your pus, your
Vile excrescences sending
Roots deep inside you.
I shall repair, redress, fix,
Cure.
And in so doing,
Allow myself my daily joy
Of playing
With blood, knife, needle and thread.
Cut, remove, stitch
With delicate gloved hands.
The sympathy,
The explanation,
The reassurance, I mean it all.
But it is all a prelude to
What must follow.
Come let us put
You to sleep for a while.
And then let me
Play.
With you. In you.
You'll feel better.
I promise.

Daisies

Every summer
On the grass verge outside my home
The daisies come up.

My daughter used to
Knot them together and make
Daisy chains.

She has left home,
Yet the daisies show up
Every summer.

Abhimanyu – a poem for Remembrance Day

It was the thirteenth day.
The sky, dull and grey with cumulus clouds
Held off from shedding a single drop,
Biding its time.
The birds that flew over the battlefield
Had all paused –
They knew a big beast would fall today.
The omens were there, if you paused to look.
A cold wind blew in from the Yamuna.

All over the vast battlefield
Through the early hours of the morning
The enemy army had taken the shape of a spiral
Inviting entry
Into a progressively narrow channel where
They could cut you down.
The chakravyūha.

Arjun was away.
By accident or design
He had been lured to a distant corner.
Only one other warrior knew how to enter this formation.
This boy of sixteen.
He knew how to go in.
Was there a way out?
He did not know.

His uncles, his kin
Gathered around.
Lead on and we will follow, they said.

We will have your back. Lead on.
He was young.
He was handsome.
He was brave.
His bow was taut.
His quiver was full of arrows.
His sword was sharp.
His horse was keen.

Trumpets blew.
Flags flapped in the morning breeze.
Elephants reared and honked.
The priests had completed their prayers.
It was time to attack.

He drove his chariot into the depth of the spiral,
Leading the charge.
Arrow after arrow flew from his bow
Felling one warrior after another.
His sword flashed at anyone that got close.
It did not matter how brave or how strong
The other man was,
This lad had his measure.
As each of the famed enemy kings
Came up and challenged him,
He beat each one back.
He was invincible.
The enemy's wheel was disintegrating.
Chaos spread.
Was the battle going to be won today?
But as the sun reached its zenith
They finally managed to
Get behind him and cut off

Those who were following.
Suddenly he was surrounded.

Seven? Eight?
He could not count how many of them
Having failed to beat him one-on-one
Bore down on him together.
Codes of honour!
Rules of combat?
All forgotten.
These men were his uncles, teachers,
Kinsmen all.
He had played on their laps
Been blessed by them on his birthdays.
They came down on him
Like a pack of feral dogs.

His bow snapped.
He took to his sword.
His sword broke.
His chariot fell apart under him.
He picked up the wheel
And used it as a shield.
But how many swords can you fend off?
They hacked him down
Their sixteen-year-old nephew.
One held his hair and pinned him down
While another drove a lance
Into his heart.

It was only then
That the rain began to fall.

They said the gods wept, when
Abhimanyu
Son of Arjun
Pride of the Pandav army
Died on the field of Kurukshetra
On the thirteenth day of battle
Murdered by his kin.

In a distant palace
His mother shivered when a gust of wind
Blew out the lamps she had lit for the deities.
She knew.
Elsewhere his young wife felt
The baby kick repeatedly.
She wondered.

As the army retreated
And regrouped that night,
Arjun wept in the firelight
Over his son's corpse,
Swore to Krishna
That he would kill each and every one of his clan
Whose swords had touched the boy.

And so he did.
From the next day
All gallantry was forgotten
All honour shelved.
This would be a battle
To utterly destroy the other.
Rarely has a battle pivoted so
On one life
One death.

That war of the Mahabharat has held many lessons
For those that have cared to learn.
One is that the best and the brightest
Die young.
Were it not for their lives
There would be no victory.

Note to self

O kind liberal
Who I see in the mirror,
Remember that
Thinking kind thoughts,
Or feeling anger at
All the injustices in the world,
Achieves nothing.
It may make you
Feel good, but
Achieves nothing.
The world remains the sodden
Mess that it is,
And you remain the privileged,
Comfortable sod
That you are.

Fireflies

You left.
I sat on our porch
Looking at the water.
Darkness fell,
And all that remained
Were the fireflies.

The world in my oven

I see icebergs melt
As butter does
In the microwave.
I see seismic upheavals
Volcanic eruptions
Faults break in the earth's surface
As cake rises.
I see forests wither
In summer heat
And catch fire.
But in the other life
There isn't my divine hand
To go in
And fix what is wrong.
No knob to dial
Down the heat.

Choices

A seed has no
Choice on where it falls
And has to take root.
In the lushest of ground
It may fail to thrive.
And yet, in dry concrete,
At the edge of a car park
Or a filling station
You will find one
Growing fiercely
Coaxing blooms
Seemingly from nothing
Saying, "Look at me
I am alive
I am beautiful."

Sixth sense

I am risk-averse
Which is why
I try not to
See you.

I sense danger.

Age

Life strips me like an onion
Layer by layer,
Year on year.
A relentless, slow diminution.
Pain infects the joints,
Nerves lose coordination.
Thoughts drop out of my head
While still forming.
Names escape me.
The heart that drove me
To mountaintops
Now falters getting through
A day in bed.
The ever-shrinking perimeter of where I go,
Is determined by helpers.
The slow withering of my beloved,
Weighed down by caring for me.
How long will this continue,
This interminable dying of the light?
And when that final tissue is breached
What will death find?
Resigned stillness? Perhaps.
Or an incandescent rage
That it had to end
Like this.

Brief encounter

Three in the afternoon
The Underground is not too crowded
A beggar comes through the train
Rattling the change in his plastic mug
Probably fifty, probably Eastern European
Spinal deformity, weak leg, crutch
Stubbly, smelly
The young man sat opposite me
Clean, muscular
Hands tucked into pockets of his hoody
Makes eye contact
With the beggar, and smiles
Apologetically as if to say
Sorry I am not giving you anything.
The beggar lights up
With a big smile
And put his hand out
For a shake.
The young man stares briefly
At the hand
Keeps his own in his pockets
And says,
"Don't touch me."
The beggar's smile fades
He pulls his hand back
Shuffles on
Rattling his mug.
The young man sits
Staring into space.

The sun always rises in Akola

The Bombay Howrah Mail –
We took that every summer
To go visit my mum's folks
In Calcutta.

The train would set off
At seven in the evening
From VT station,
Leaving behind crowds and cacophony.
My brother and I, excited
Staring out of the window,
Our brains thrumming to the rhythm of the train.

Soon food would get unpacked
We would eat
Holdalls would be unrolled
Berths flipped open
And we would be tucked into bed
Still excited
Not wanting to sleep.

The next morning, inevitably
As I climbed down from my berth
And looked out of the window
The sun would be rising over fields
Vast, orange
And the train would pull into Akola.

Whenever I see the sun rise, wherever on earth
I am the boy in that train again.
And it is Akola.

Mentors

Every surgeon I've worked with
Has taught me a thing or two
How to do something well
And sometimes, how not to.

There isn't any one person
Who I would rather be
Like a magpie I've stolen bits of each
To make what passes as me.

Honeybee

You fly about all day
In the sun, and capture
The essence of sunshine.

I don't know how many trips you made
To how many flowers
In which valley or glade
To make this sticky amber.

As the stolen fruit
Of your labour dissolves
On my tongue,
All I can think, is
Thank you.

In the Shower

You may just have a quick fag
Or you may score a high
You may choose to cut yourself
On the inside of your thigh
You may give yourself pleasure
By stroking a certain bit
You may stick a finger in your throat
And make yourself vomit
You might have a nice warm shower
And towel yourself dry
Or you might simply want to turn
The water on and cry

Autumn

The days are getting shorter
Summer is on the run
Our part of the earth
Has swung away from the sun

The mornings start off misty
The wind feels really cool
I get goosebumps on my legs
As I wait for the bus to school

Fat peaches in my snack box
Eat them quickly, can't take too long
For in the recess we practise
Our harvest festival song

The evenings get dark quickly
I can't go out to play
Grandpa grumbles about how cold it is
While Dad rakes the leaves away

Ma and Grandma cook sweets in the kitchen
Dassera has just begun
Diwali and Halloween are yet to come
Autumn will be fun!

Kihim afternoon

The air is still
Not a ripple on the surface of the pool
Woodsmoke in my nostrils
A bird calls like a metronome in the distance
Sparrows chatter, crows bicker
Ants scurry with fragments of food
A fly settles lazily on me
I wait for when you will wake.

Futility?

All my life I have
Chased shadows.
The tumours I cut out
Often destined
To return
And kill.
The bodies
I have healed
Doomed to crumble away over time.

India

There she was
Warm, wild, rich beyond measure
Protected by fools
Who knew not what they held.
You saw your chance, you took her
God, you took her!

You used her
Stole her wealth
Her children you enslaved
The ones who protested
You strangled.

Oh, some of you
Did love her
Loved her children
Studied her
But use her you all did.

Don't tell me
And don't delude yourselves
That it was an act
Of kindness.
You left only when you had to.

Your palaces still stand.
She is just getting
Off her knees.

Jahar's room, on the anniversary of his death

A sparse, bare room.
A thin layer of dust coats it all.
Books on the lives of saints
Hindu philosophy
All neatly covered with brown paper
With his name and the year
Written on the front pages.
His shawl
His umbrella
His bed
His slippers
Some Good Knight mosquito coils.
A year has gone by.
His photo is already fading on the wall.
But today a fresh garland hangs on it.

Ambulance

As I drive through city traffic, slowly it draws near,
A shiny reminder of our transience – I pull over to leave the way clear
I wonder who it's taking where, and what might the matter be
It carries a whisper of déjà vu, wakes a distant memory
There was a time, another day, in a van just like that
I lay looking at my ECG trace, hoping it wouldn't go flat
I made it that day, as did the crew that carried me
Though icy city streets to the hospital where I needed to be
They worked on me, the cath lab lot, skilfully and fast
Unblocked that artery quickly, put in a stent that would last
I've lived to fight another day, to love, to laugh, to dance
Oh, it's a wonderful thing, to be given a second chance
So, make haste good ambulance, with your precious cargo,
In your battle to save that life, you just get one go.

Vincent

Your world
Is all around me.
The spirals of clouds in
Your skies.
The stars in the night.
The bright sun on
Haystacks,
Cornfields.
Trains chugging past suburbs.
Cherry blossoms
Fruit and bread on tables.
Sunflowers in vases.
And irises.
Postmen and potato farmers.
Cafes.
Asylums.

The hungry look
In your sunken eyes.
Prominent cheekbones
Gaunt face.
Red stubble.
Hair cropped short.

You did not have the money
To buy paint or brushes.
What made you spend
Your entire life
Painting canvases
That no one would buy?

What were you trying to say?
"What have I done to deserve this?
Why can I see the beauty
In my work but
You cannot?"

My spirit reaches out
To you over time
To give you a hug.
I smell the tobacco and beer
On your jacket,
The turpentine on your brushes.

I am so grateful, Vincent
So grateful.

Dusk

"It is at Dusk that the most interesting things occur,
for that is when simple differences fade away.
I could live in everlasting Dusk,"
Says a character of
Olga Tokarczuk.
When I think dusk
I see the sun
Set over Shivaji Park.
The kids pull up their cricket stumps
And wander home.
Shoppers crowd the vegetable markets.
Glary fluorescent lights go on in flats.
And the smell of evening cooking
Wafts out.

End of summer

If go I must
Let me go in September.
There will still be warmth in the air.
The last swallows of summer will still be around
The morning sun will still flood the back garden
The last roses will bloom
There will be a pile of apples to bake into tarts
There will be concerts in the park
And the last games of cricket
Yes, if go I must
Let me go in September.

Glass ceiling

I don't see the glass ceiling.
Never have,
Thus far.

Or maybe
I am deluded.
It is there,
Right above me,
All the time,
And I don't see it.
It is a glass ceiling
After all.

Can I tell you all
Who are making that
Ceiling for me,
I have superpowers.
All I need to do
Is take a deep breath,
Wrap my cape around me
Push my fist up
And fly,

Crash my way up
Through your
Glass ceiling.

Ha!

Holiday destination

Come all ye moneyed people
You rich and glamorous ones
Come to our desert paradise
Spend money and have some fun

We have roads as wide as any
And buildings very tall
Hotels that are so, so comfy
And the world's largest mall

You may not find much culture here
But you will find us very nice
Anything your heart desires
We will deliver in a trice

We used to trade in dates and pearls
But these days we sell gold
The measure of a man with us
Is what he's bought and sold

Repressed? We may be a bit
And a bit repressive too
But hey, don't dwell on our faults
Let's show you what we can do

So, come to our pleasure beaches
Soak up the winter sun
Come to our desert paradise
Spend money and have some fun

There is a bright star in the sky tonight

We see the couple knocking on the door
Begging shelter, to just sleep on the floor.
They've travelled from afar, we don't know how
She's heavily pregnant, may birth right now.
So, what shall we do tonight, let them stay?
Clean up the manger and spread out the hay?
Can we not afford this, are we not able
To have two more mouths tonight at our table?

But these strangers who today beg a hand
Will tomorrow want a piece of your land.
They are not your problem, don't you see?
Let them in and tomorrow they will be.
Be sensible, keep them out, see the obvious danger.
Go to bed, making sure you've properly locked the manger.

Same/Not

It is never the same wave
Never the same cloud
Same sky though
And the same ocean
Never the same people either

To K

When I lie back in the dark
And think of you
My face always breaks
Into a smile

End of CPR

Life passes
Like water through your fingers.

The life you are trying so hard
To save,
Slips away
Amidst the beeping of the monitor
Despite the jolt
Of the defibrillator.

The warmth goes
Rapidly.

Fever

My beautiful, beautiful girl child
There was a time when
Your hand slipped into mine
Instinctively when we crossed
The road, or
The room darkened.

Now in this dark room
My face turns to you.
Your fingers feel cool
On my fevered forehead.

Taj Mahal

Hubris, was it?
Or a desire to create
Something exquisite?
We all love,
But a marble pile we do
Not make to remind
Us daily of our
Lost beloveds.

But what a pile!
The gorgeous form
The aching symmetry
Cool white marble
Lapis and cornelian.
The river behind.
Shallow pools and
Tall trees in front.
And antlike,
Noisy,
Half of humanity!
It should have been
Just the breeze
The birds
And the murmur
Of the water.
Instead we have this
Gentle clamour
Rise over the stone

My fourth time here
And yet it enchants

Valentine's Day

I look at you
My darling one
And think of the times we've had together
Times of grief, times of fun.

We've walked together
Hand in hand
Down many a street
In many a land

We keep messing in the kitchen together
Rustling up a dish
You don't ever eat it
But you cook me meat and fish.

We've built a home together
Brought up our girl
The years have gone by
In a wonderful dizzying whirl

We haven't made millions
Frittered pounds away
But a good bottle of red counts more than money
At the end of a hospital day.

I haven't got you roses each day
Or poured you champagne
In fact, I know very well
I have often been a pain

You're grumpy too
Nag me to death
Will that ever change?
I'm not holding my breath!

Our bodies are creaking a bit
Bits are falling off
But you can still hold your downward dog
While I am nodding off.

But love you madly
That I do
And I'll say it again today
I love you.

Nocturne

The light fades.
Darkness spreads like a stain
Through the trees.
Turning browns and greens
To blue and then black.

Toil ends.
Stocktaking done.
Birds return to nests
Bees to hives.
Stars show up.

In the undergrowth
Creatures stir, go about
Seeking food and warmth.
Drops of water fall
From leaves to the forest floor.
Mist rises

It has been thus for centuries
Before you and I.

This soil has absorbed
Fallen leaves
Dead insects, birds
Animal and human bodies
And yet remained
The soft dark sponge that
Soaks up the dew today.

The salmon's dream

The water is full of scales and dirt
Food gets dropped in twice a day.
As he flaps around exercising his
Flabby muscles
In the wire cage
With a hundred others
The caged salmon dreams.

He is the king
He has done roaming the ocean
He is headed home
He remembers nothing of it
But he knows it is home
The smell of it in the water
Pulls him along
His brothers and sisters
Are with him
They run through the bays
Where orcas hunt in packs
And sea serpents lurk
Past Humpback Corner
Into the river mouth
Upstream
His sinews ripple
He jumps rapids
He skims through reeds
Dodges nets
Flies past bears
He is headed home.

Mirror

My best friend lives in a mirror down the hallway
We say "Hello" to each other a few times each day
We're the same age and build, but he looks a lot older
Right now we're both nursing a rather painful shoulder
He's a shy chap –- hides whenever I'm looking away.

Solitude

Evening in an alien city
Lights go on
Music floats out of bars.
People hurry home.
Behind closed doors
They will be laughing, kissing
Sitting down to dinner.
I feel strangely bereft
That I have nowhere
To go, no one
To meet.

April 2020/pandemic

This spring is bountiful
And cruel.
Coaxing blooms out of buds
And life
Out of lungs.

A reason for stasis

Go on an adventure.
In that phrase, the key word
Is go.
You have to leave here.
The implications of that departure
The things you will not do
Who you will leave
What that will do to them,
And to you,
Is what stops you.

Brook

I know not which hillside you've come from
I know not where you will end
Subsumed into a river
All I am doing is crossing you
As down my pointless path I wend.

The water is clear, with a hint of peat
Algae and weeds wave their tresses
In the dappled sunlight I see
Little silver fish dart around
Under moss-covered rocks and dark recesses

Leaves, little white blossoms
Fall into the water and float along
Just above me I can hear
A single robin trill
Copying your gurgles in his song

Insects take off as I approach
Some small furry creature scurries away
The breeze carries a blush of warmth
On these stones I could sit
And spend the rest of my day

I shall of course get up and leave
Just as that robin will take flight
Over the stones that I am stepping on
Deer will cross during the day
And, I'm sure, foxes in the night

May you stay here, in your course
For years, for probably as long
As there is life on earth
May another human, years hence,
Pause just like me, to hear your song

The last station

There is a perfection in death
A journey complete.
No more struggles, doubts, fears
No more errors to repeat.
Friends, foes, family can
Make their summations
Commend my works
Criticise my omissions.
My one regret is the
Grief that will be
Theirs who – alas –
Might still love me.

Neurotransmitters

There are days when my mind
Shuns poetry.
I don't want to write
Or read even.
And then, on other days,
Words intoxicate me.
Lines flow.
I wonder what this rhythm is.
Is it just work?
Is it the level of some chemical
In my brain synapses?

Human affairs

The affairs of men seem to be run by
The rich and the powerful on the sly.
They will make a covert deal, sign a secret deed
Their actions, somehow, always driven by greed
Never by charity, altruism or fairness.
And all the rest of life just falls into harness –
The apparatus of the state, legal frameworks,
The creators of news, sell those decisions to us
So that we accept them unquestioningly and pay
Literally and metaphorically, to our dying day.
The pity is that humanity, and with us all
This planet's creatures great and small
Will pay the price for the greed of the wealthy few
And the acquiescence of us who know not what to do.

Conversation over dinner

A lady who I barely know
Sits next to me at a dinner
And amidst the banalities of chatter
She suddenly says to me,
"Surely the Empire was a force for good?"

It sounds like a question from her, not an assertion.
Is she naive? Is she a fool?
Is she shrewder than I think
And seeking the measure of me?
Is this the time or place for a serious discussion?

What am I to say to her?
That all empires are built on violence?
That this lovely hall we are sat in
Was somehow built because my ancestors
Stood knee-deep in paddy fields?

"I guess you can find some good
In anything, if you look hard enough,"
I say with a shrug and a smile.
That seems to do.
And we concentrate on the pudding.

On the wings of words

The hands that held on firmly
To the train leaving the station
The feet that walked me through
Endless corridors of airport terminals
Are now painful and weak.

My body, my passport to the universe,
Is now – alas – my prison.
I can now travel to distant lands
Only through words, through poems
That light up the television screen of my mind.

To surgeons – on craft

We know how to wield a knife.
That moment of destiny
When knife touches skin
And the first drop of blood wells out.
We know that thrill.
We share that knowledge.

I have learnt from my masters.
I am passing it on to my apprentices
They will too, in their time.
In this world of craft
You and I know a master
When we see one.

It is not how many papers you have written
Or posts held, or money made, gongs bestowed
Or what you post on Twitter
That earns you the respect of your peers.
It is what you do each day
To the tissues you splice open and put together,
How well you do it.

We know how to wield a knife.

Gazofilacio

Clive James mentioned this word
That means the treasure chambers of the mind
It echoes the Bengali phrase Smritir monikotha
I wonder what would my treasure box contain?

It would be shaped like the brass box
In which my grandmother
Kept her accessories for eating paan.
There would be a tray with little compartments
And in them would be snatches of music

The first time I heard Apu's theme from Pather Panchali,
I was Apu walking down that path.
And the first time I heard Bach's Cello Suites,
Played by Rostropovich.
On headphones, in the middle of the night
In a hotel room in New York,
In a few concentrated hours
I felt yet again
The joy of being human.
Vivaldi's Four Seasons
Playing in a Venetian church,
Playing anywhere.
McCartney saying to me,
In the midst of despair,
"Let it be."
Bhimsen Joshi's voice taking off in a concert
Starting from his navel
Emerging through his throat
Flying over the rooftops.

Fiddle music that people were dancing to
In a Dublin pub.
Scott Joplin on a Sunday afternoon.
The entire crowd in Geeta Cinema in Worli
Clapping in rhythm to every song
In a rerun of Baiju Bawra.
A Baul singing to his ektara
On a train going to Birbhum.
Sonos filling every room in my house
With Meera's bhajans
In Vani Jairam's dusky voice.
And Tagore. Always Tagore.
Or Robi Thakur as I think of him.
Song after song after song.
A song for every moment
For every emotion.
From dark chords of deep sorrow
To the simple joy of walking in a sunlit rice field.

My treasure box is filling up.

September 2020

Saffron is the colour now
Faded are the green and white
If you're not the kind they want you to be
You had better stay out of sight
The one you think is the saviour
His right hand is the knave
The land I knew is dead and gone
It's rotting in its grave

Wisdom

He came once, the Grim Reaper, and said "Hello"
On a winter's morning ten years past
But then, on a sudden whim, he chose to let go
I don't know how long this reprieve might last

Since then I have tried to be wise
Treated each day as though it might be my last
Made my bed, called mother, tried to see the sunrise
And when at night I have held you fast
To myself I have repeated this quiet refrain
It's okay if I never wake up to see your face again

Bitter tears

The fire is dead.
Dead are the children
Of the revolution.
The best and the brightest
Are always the first to die.

The ones who fled
Kept quiet,
Or turned traitor,
They rule the roost now,
Wield power, act virtuous.

To forget their cowardice,
They erase the brave
From talk, from print, from film.
Old comrades see it
But have learnt to hold silent.

But the mothers remember.
You will see them in the square
Where they meet to reminisce,
Shed bitter tears
And share dreams of revenge.

Don't!

Old flames
Old haunts
People or places you remember fondly –
Best to let those memories be
And not visit them again
In the flesh.
All you will see are
Changes wrought by time,
Usually for the worse.
An inevitable corruption.
The warm memories of yesterday
Postulations of what might have been
Will be replaced by
Your knowledge of the disappointing
Here and now.

Mstislav

Your cello –
It speaks to me
As clear as a human voice

Baba

Three years.
Three years now that you have gone
And yet the wound feels raw.

As I look every morning at the dawn sky
I remember you telling me
To look every morning at the dawn sky.

Snatches of songs,
The smell of something cooking,
A new film that you would have loved,

Leafing through a book on my shelves
That you gave me on a birthday,
A bowl of lychees…

You had a long, fulfilled life.
I must grieve and move on.
All that – I know.

You have left your gentle mark
On me, and I don't just mean
My Y chromosome.

I feel that imprint still,
Every day.
Never knew I would miss you so.

Offspring

Having writ your poems
You look at them again and again
With trepidation

You tweak, you prune
You adjust the rhythm
Topiary comes to mind

You hold them for a while
But there must come a time
To let them go

To let them fly
Meet others
Be loved, criticised, derided

You don't raise children
To keep them locked up in the house
For the rest of their lives

Autumn morning conversation

The weather is awful, windy and wet
Go for a walk now? No way!
Let's make ourselves some hot chocolate
And crawl back under that warm duvet.

This virus!
How it came to be among us
We do not know.
We do not know what to do about it.
Close bars? Open bars?
Eat out? Or not?
Fly? Or not?
Congregate? Isolate?
Wear masks? Where?
Our leaders reveal themselves
As the fools we thought they weren't.
As we shut down in fear
Thousands die of disease anyway
Millions starve.
Come on humankind –
The initial bumbling,
The missteps,
I can understand.
But surely now, after months,
We need to have a clear plan
For how to deal with this.
And more important
This virus is holding up a mirror
To everything that is wrong
With how we treat each other
And the rest of the planet.
Are we so blind that we cannot
See the picture
And act?

To the conifers behind my house

While I am your custodian
I shall be just that –
Look after you.

I shall not be here forever
Nor will you
Though you will probably outlast me.

But the transience of all life
Does not make it meaningless.
Instead, it adds
To the importance of this moment
The blue sky and the sun
Shining on my face through
Your branches.
This, here and now,
Is a wonderful treasure.

* * *

As I spend an hour picking up
A huge mass of pine cones and needles
From my kitchen roof
I think – clearing someone's droppings
Human, animal or plant
Is surely an expression
Of love.

Icaria

They say Icaria is the place to be
If you wish to live past four score, or five
A bright green speck in an iridescent sea
Made famous by the winged man's dive

The good folks there live a simple life
Fish, farm, tend herds, in bright sunshine
Quiet days, free of stress and strife
Meals of bread, olives, fish, washed down with some wine.

Cars there are few in number
The people just walk everywhere
Their hearts beat long, their arteries are clean
Their lungs are full of fresh air.

You and I have complex lives,
Work through days long and drab
We have rush hour commutes all through town
Money to make and backs to stab.

We exercise on treadmills
The sun we barely see
Meals are hastily eaten sandwiches
Washed down with cups of coffee.

Our children turn into nervous wrecks
Our spouses are disenchanted
By the time we are forty-five
Angina is taken for granted.

What's keeping you my friend
From leaving here, and going to Icaria?
Or better still, why don't we
Begin to build an Icaria here?

Oh, don't be a cynic,
Let's give this a try
Before you and I both
Fall, burning, from the sky.

Louise Glück

This is not an excuse.
I am a modestly read man
And I did not even know of you
Until you won The Prize.

As I read your verses now
I find that your words linger
In the echo chamber of my mind
With growing resonance.

Your poems fill me with hope
That this craft – of writing –
Is worthwhile
And that this life is worth living.

A song for the NHS

A brown envelope on my doorstep
What might it be? Let me guess
Yes, just as I thought
It is my P45 from the NHS!

Thirty-one years
That's how long it's been
I was but a young registrar
When I arrived on the scene.

Fresh out of training in India
An intense lad with a moustache, and thick hair
A prelude to today's spectacled me
With my grey, respectable air

I came here to train and learn more
Did that for six years and went back too
But private medicine in a city there
Wasn't really what I wanted to do.

'Twas the NHS that proved to be my real home
It drew me back, with fresh commitments
Made me move, yet again,
At great trouble, across continents

The years since have gone
Like a rapid slide show – of operating,
Rounding, consulting, teaching,
Lecturing, researching and writing.

Holding hands, holding knives, holding lives!
Offering tissues, band-aids, cups of tea
And thanks to vending machines
Drinking too many abysmal cups of coffee

Snatches of sleep in theatre between cases
Early morning alarms before the break of light
Calling Mum in India while driving to work
Crashing into bed, dog-tired, late at night

Bleeps, pagers and phone calls
Have ruled my days and nights
The only times I have switched off
Were when I was on flights!

As operations have dragged on
Well past my working day
I have missed many a birthday,
Anniversary and school play.

The family have been always kind
Forgiven this perennial sinner
Though the missus does get rather cross
When my phone goes off at dinner.

I have looked after amazing people
Kind, gracious, grateful, ever so brave
And my other family have been my
Workmates, my fellow slaves!

The care I gave was set
In crowded, grubby shabbiness
Sometimes slow, mired in
Bureaucratic sloppiness

But always with true heart
And usually top-class.
Anywhere in the world, any scrutiny
This would pass

I cannot understand those who say
With "state" care they wouldn't bother
Care that is free is the greatest
Gift we can give each other

The ones who say that are often
American, and always rather wealthy
The truth that stares them in the face
They prefer not to see.

Glass ceilings? I haven't seen any
And maybe broken a few
What mattered were my actual skills
Never my original hue.

I am leaving tired and worn out
Happy to walk away
But I don't think I would have
Wanted it any other way

I don't know, once I have left
How much I am going to miss
These days of toil, frustration, achievement
And – often – bliss

I know I might still keep working
In venues nicer, more glossy
Will they match my NHS years?
I'll just have to wait and see.

Imperfection

Husbands always fall short.
I know I do,
In so many ways
In all the roles I play –
Let's not even go there.

May I submit that those
Are forgivable lapses.
There are things I do
Very well, too.
Of which I know you are proud.

But it is not your measure
Of a good husband
That I really aspire to,
But your measure
Of a good man.

Lockdown #2/November 2020

A bleak winter looms
A masked ball
Of death
Deprivation
And depression

A surgeon, on baking

Yet again, it is something
I do
With my hands.
But nothing bleeds.
There is no life-
Or-death question.
No one hurts.

Popat

On a bright autumn morning
In my suburban garden,
Three parakeets descend.
Feathers of bright green
Among the maples and pines.
Raucous chatter.

In a flash they remind me
Of warm summer afternoons
In India.

Note from a tree

Imagine you are rooted to one spot.
You have arms. Many.
But they are fixed.
You cannot move them around.
You might sway passively in the wind
But you don't move.

Movement is overrated, I think –
My life comes to me.

You can grow though.
Slowly.
Towards light.
Away from the wind
Or the shadow.
You have lots of fingers
Or say feathers
And more grow every spring
But they all fall away
In the cold.
Are you beginning to get a feel
For what it means to be me?

I know very well where I am
I know who are around me.
I know how deep the aquifer is.
I know from which direction the sun rises
And when.

There are bits of me
That are very attractive
To insects
My flowers grow each summer
Whether I want them or not
Like acne.
I can sense
The bees, flies, caterpillars
Coming, flitting, buzzing
Sipping my juices
Flying away, scurrying away.
And my fruit!
Birds, bats, insects, humans
They all want my fruit.

I sense the others around me.
My roots build intricate castles
That you cannot see.
I know where the moles and rabbits are.
Every one mushroom, every earthworm.
I know every creature that pauses in my shade
I know every bird that nests on me,
Or rests.
Every ant, every butterfly,
Every human – the ones who climb me
The ones who rest beneath
The ones who cut and prune.
My neighbour trees that my roots touch
And sometimes my branches too
The ones who send me messages.

I suffer the rain.
I suffer the cold.
I suffer when it is too dry.
But I sense the warmth in the air
The direction of the sun
I drink deep from the earth
I soak up goodness from the loam.
That fulfils me.
I love the insects coming to me
I am happy when the cows pause
To rest in my shade.
I watch the birds build their nests
Feed their babies
The babies fly away.
I am happy
When the petals fall,
When the wind
Blows the dead leaves off me.
I love my fruits being eaten
By those who visit.

I am alive.
I am content.
Come, sit beneath me.

The traitor within

It lurks, quiet, in a dark recess,
Oblivious of night or day.
Slowly pushing soft tentacles forward
Through the thickets of soft undergrowth.
Grabbing more turf,
Seducing neighbours to bring it food.
Growing, breeding, shedding,
Coaxing its offspring to go forth and germinate.
Silently weaving its plan of world domination.

Opposites

What is meat and sustenance to me
To you is murder of the innocents
My days of creative writing are
To you, waste paper, worth ten cents.
You spout the virtues of conservatism
And I say you are evil.
When I talk of social equity
To you I am the devil.
You still want to travel and see
All the wild places.
I can't be bothered to budge from the sofa
And do up my bootlaces.
It looks like if there's one thing
On which we agree at all
It's that on a winter afternoon
Nothing beats hot rice and dahl.

Home (1)

Home sits deep in my head
I can go there
Whenever I wish.

When I drive down the motorway
Or lie awake in bed at dawn
I quickly open a window and look in.

There pedlars walk down narrow lanes
In the late afternoon
Calling out their wares.

Friends come to the door
And ask, "Won't you come
Out to play?"

Green and yellow mangoes
Sit in wooden crates
Lined with straw.

The smell of Ma's cooking wafts in the air.
The smell of Ma
When I bury my face in her lap.

Grandma gives me her mortar and pestle
To mash her betel leaves
So she can chew them without her dentures.

I splash into the pond
With my brother
The ripples reach the lotuses at the far end.

Let that mouse be?

There is a little mouse in my garden
A rather silly one, in fact
When I loom upon him, he thinks
To sit and cower is an evasive act.

The thing with vermin is that they too want to live
To raise their children, to last beyond tomorrow.
The trouble with weeds is no one told them
They are weeds. They keep wanting to grow.

On poets

I read the works of others, wordsmiths far superior
Sometimes it is the thoughts that amaze
But often it is the way they have put them down
The words, the rhythms, the interplays, the turns of phrase
And I am filled with awe and wonder,
And a deep sense of inadequacy.

Religion

A believer I am not.
I think God is a construct of clever humans
Who want the rest to behave
As they think we should;
Who control us
And profit from us.

When my daughter was little
She always carried with her
A soft piece of flannel
She called it her "Jiji".
God is the Jiji
For all believers –
Their security blanket
Illogical, but warm and comforting.

Yet, the brook in the mountains
The morning sky
The pebble on the beach
They can hold me for hours
And I wonder
Surely there must be more than this?

From this genuine wonder
To the throngs that worship at the temple
With their prayers of transaction.
That journey is like the one
A river makes
From a clear stream in the hills
To a pungent flow of molasses
Drifting into the sea.

Birthday thoughts

Good morning, earth.
Yes, I am still here.
Still feeling that I have a purpose,
That I serve a purpose.
Still feeling well.
Still feeling loved.
Now, that is a lot of positives!

There is no significance to this day.
The planet has merely done one more tour
Around the sun
Since little, insignificant me
Popped out
No doubt to my mother's great relief and joy.

I am lucky it is a holiday today.
Today is a day to pause,
To go for a walk in the park,
To unwrap gifts,
Eat well,
Enjoy being with the family.
Take stock.
Make plans.
Small plans. Big plans.
Have things to look forward to.
To be grateful.
To be happy.

Morning round

He came by, the consultant,
Said my tumours had grown.
They were actually much bigger
Than the recent scans had shown.

They couldn't cut them out
When they went in yesterday.
They decided, chemo first,
Maybe surgery another day.

Sometimes tumours shrink with chemo
And then oft times they don't.
Worse than what he said to me
Was the bit that he won't.

The nurse looks on with kindly eyes
I wonder what she is thinking?
What did those on the Carpathia think
When they saw the Titanic sinking?

It's a bright August morning outside
The traffic's roaring by
I'm lying here wondering
Is he saying I'm going to die?

My life is a fistful of sand
Slowly falling away.
People will say, "Make the best you can
Of each remaining day."

Well, who really cares if I live or die
Does anyone give a shit?
My parents will be broken, friends will cry
And then that will be it.

Futile, futile, futile
The pointlessness of it all.
Why was I born, why did I live
So far, to take this fall?

Twenty-eight is rather young to die
Most people will admit,
But that's all I have got to go
If this cancer won't remit.

My mouth is dry, my tummy hurts,
I need to get on with my day.
I've got a lot of battling to do
If my cancer is here to stay.

Bring on the fucking mindfulness
And the anti-emetic drip,
I'll give my fate as good as I get
On what may be my final trip.

Into the wild

The gods are retreating
Deeper into the wild.
You know they dwell
Only where the air is pure
And the water runs clear
And the wild things do
What wild things do.
They are running out of space, though.
How long do you think it will be
Before they turn around in wrath
And do what they do?

Close encounter

Of that moment when my heart stopped
I remember but three things.

The crushing pain in my chest
That brought tears to my eyes.

My thought – What? So soon? Is it time to go?

And my daughter holding my hand.

Disco

Come, fill my world
With a wall of sound
Get my feet tapping
And take me back to my youth.
When I wore flares
And everything was possible
And I looked shyly at her
Across the dance floor

Fields

This is where it has come to.
An overcast sky
An autumn day
A wheat field that extends to the horizon
Utterly flat, harvested, etched
With evenly spaced parallel lines
No bird. No insect.
Just silence.
I have just seen mankind's epitaph.
It is kind.
It says,
"They knew not what they did."

In the OR

I am but a bookish nerd
Not very fit at all
Almost anyone will outwrestle me
Or run faster with a ball.
I am tired if I walk a bit
Yoga taxes me
If I had to pick a sport for myself
I'd pick origami

But put me in the OR
With a knife in my hand
And I am suddenly a different man
In a totally different land.
I am Genghis Khan riding into battle
At the head of my marauding horde.
I am a samurai warrior, putting
The world to rights with my sword.
I am Maverick up in the clouds
Swapping fire with the enemy.
I am the captain of my ship
Sailing a turbulent sea.
No adventure you can ever imagine
No storm, cyclone or fire
Beats what I do every day of my life
With my scalpel in the OR.

Up and down

There was a young, adventurous adder
Who, being curious, went up a ladder
But no sooner than he had ascended
He very rapidly descended
As he had to urgently empty his bladder

Rules for the Canadian wilderness

Never ever say "Boo" to caribous
Do not share booze with a moose
Mind your own affairs
And in deference to bears
Always wear good running shoes

Waves

You are walking up the beach
Right at the water's edge
As the waves come in they gently lap at your feet
The warm water feels good
Your eye is on the horizon
Your mind is elsewhere
Suddenly comes a big wave
Out of nowhere
That hits you
Splat!
Wets you to the waist.

This keeps happening
And not only at the water's edge.

Finding love

Love is not just laughter and roses
Or meaningful glances and touching of hands
Or sunlit meadows and summer pollen
And riverbanks where cormorants sun.
Nor is it dancing cheek to cheek
Or nights of passion under linen sheets.

We found love amid
The smells of disinfectant and pus
Crowded wards of sweaty breathless bodies
Drawing up injections swiftly to stop cries of pain
Passing tubes into suicidal stomachs
To wash out poison
Operating through the night
Opening one foetid belly after another.
Reading side by side
Buried in books late on nights off
Riding high on cups of tea
Yes, that is where I found you
And you found me.

Early morning

There are times when you awaken
Before the alarm has gone.
And you optimistically think to yourself
It is still dark
I can go back to sleep.
And then, as you stare
Bleary-eyed into the
Lightening dark,
You hear the hint of birdsong
That gets through the double glazing.

Time to suppress a sigh
And get up.

Gratitude

You find gratitude
In the strangest of places.

The ones I have nurtured
With a lot of deliberation and thought
Have the attitude that a sapling
May have for the gardener.
"He planted me?
So what? Did he have a choice?"
"He watered me?
Even if he hadn't, the rain would have done the job!"
"He pruned me?
Well, that hurt like hell."

The ones I cared for because it was my job,
And the ones I didn't even know I was doing anything for,
They are the ones.
They are the ones who remind me
Year on year
That my job has been worth doing.

The ones I nurtured
Ah, I wish them well.

Gusts

The lamps are blowing out one by one
As they inevitably will.
These gusts will still blow awhile.
Brace yourself, wrap up warm
And cherish the light that still holds.

New Year's Day, 2021

The wreath on the front door
Has the red plastic gloss on the cherries
Splitting in the cold.
Inside, the Christmas tree, now shorn
Of the bags of presents at its base,
Its harvest gone, stands
Bereft, shedding needles, waiting
For the trip to the sawmill.
Peering out of the window, I see
A grey sky
A thin layer of frost covers the rooftops
Not a car goes down the street for several minutes.
A robin and two coal tits are at the bird feeder
Looking quiet and sombre, taking turns.

The cell phone has many messages –
Friends, relatives all over
All saying the same
"Wish you a happy New Year".
One sends a picture of a queue
Forming at the temple outside her door
People huddling together
Few masks in sight.

As one door in time shuts
Behind us, another opens ahead.
Where will it take us though?

What a year this has been!

I see the human parable as a bunch of
Children on a picnic in the woods.
There are no adults to restrain us.
The woods were lovely and boundless
And there were other creatures around.
We children have managed to spend all day
Bumbling around – we think – quite happily.
But we have, unknowingly, as children often are
Been utterly cruel to each other
And to the creatures around us.
We have managed to set off fires
We have killed many of the beasts.
Killed many of us.

Now, as dusk draws near
Fires burn in several corners
The animals have fled.
We seek shelter from the flames
That we ourselves have lit
And don't know what to do.
Gradually an awareness has dawned
That these woods are finite
That we have nowhere else to go
That we ought not to kill the other creatures
That we need to be kind to each other
That this fire we have lit is deadly.
This is no picnic.

But will that wisdom help us
Weather this night?

Let us and wait and see.

I draw a deep breath in
And shuffle off to put the kettle on.

There are days

There are days
When the knife cuts sharper
The wrist feels more supple
Even the arteries bleed less
When every knot snugs down as it should
When you think you've been at it for six hours
But actually it's only three
Yes, there are days like that!

Tulips

Does a flower itself, have a sense of
Why it was born? Why does it exist?
These orange tulips now gracing my vase
Grew in a hothouse somewhere.
Planted for profit,
Cut early,
Tied into bundles,
Sent in a refrigerated truck,
Passportless but legal immigrants,
To a supermarket shelf
And thence to my living room.

There was perhaps an expectation in their petals
That there would be sunlight,
There would be wind.
There would be sap rising from the earth.
There would bees flying in
Fluffing up their pollen
And flying off
So that somewhere, later, another bulb
Would come into being.

That would have brought meaning, perhaps, to their existence.
Instead all they have had is tap water
In a sterile vase, in a sealed room.
A wasted life, as the lives of flowers go?
I guess, to them
The joy they have brought me
These few days of winter
Doesn't count at all.

To my tumour – before the second cycle of chemo

The time has come Mein Herr
For round number two.
I've got some more medicine
Specially lined up for you.

Round one wasn't bad at all,
I have no bruises to show.
You my friend on the other hand
Are already beginning to slow.

I will dance like a butterfly
And sting you like a bee,
Your cells will shrivel further
As we shall soon see.

If you think you'll pop up
Like dandelion heads on my lawn,
I am getting my giant blower out --
Very soon you'll be gone.

Sunshine

Mrs B is sitting in the winter sunshine.
In the late morning this balcony
Of her second-floor flat
Gets a lot of sun.
She is rubbing coconut oil into her skin.
Her skin is soft, like vellum in places,
Elsewhere softly crinkled like parchment.
The oil feels good on it.
A shame there isn't something that would reach so easily
Into the insides of her body
To the part metal hip that hurts every day.

The sound of city traffic rumbles in the background
But there are some crows making a louder racket
In the tree opposite.
They sometimes come and drink
From the dish of water she puts out on the ledge.
And sparrows too.
There are some plants in pots, enjoying the sun.
Hibiscus, basil, money plant.
She has just watered them.

The newspaper is by her feet, already read.
The mobile phone is on her lap
Not that she is expecting anyone to call
Both sons have called already this morning.
They are where they are.
Life is what it is.

When Mr B was alive

Especially the latter years when he was unwell
Her days had been busy.
Since he has gone
Things are so much quieter.
And now this lockdown...!

The late morning holds a promise
Of idleness
Of a shower later
And a lunch that the maid is cooking.

Mrs B pours another dollop of oil
Into her palm.
The sun feels good.

The old man and the sea

We used to row out after dusk
Young men in the moonlight
Out to the open sea
With the stars mapping the way
To where the shore was a memory, but
We knew where the shoals were

The nets were cast
And drawn in
Sleek writhing streaks of silver
In their hundreds
Slowly turning to a twitchy mass
Of blood, slime, scales and flesh
As air burnt their gills.

On the way back
The talk would be of the price of
Fish and toddy.
As we came in at dawn
The women would be on the sand
To sort and take away the catch
To sell at the market.

Then it would be time to pick one's way
Between the lines of salted fish
Hung out to dry
Back to the hut,
Finish off the rice and fish
Left on the stove
And curl up next to the sleeping children
As they stirred gently in their dreams.

Those were the days!
There were fish in the sea.
Joints were supple,
The wife was still young,
The children too small to talk back,
The toddy didn't cause heartburn,
The beedis were cheap.
Yes, those were the days.

Calcutta 1975

The acrid smell of tear gas fills the air
As the police move in with their batons
The crowd starts to fall back

On a quieter street, bullets are fired
Deliberately, at two young men
Stood up against a wall.
Blood and grey matter add
A fresh splash of red to the graffiti
"China's Chairman is our Chairman"

Ponds choked with water hyacinths
Are great places to throw bodies into –
They cover all manners of sin.

Pace

In the vast chemistry lab of life
Your life and mine are stood up like burettes,
The stopcock in each set to drip at a steady pace
Until it runs dry.
Yet why does it seem that sometimes you live a lot
Very quickly,
And at other times
It feels unending?

Reverence

You won a war.
Your statue stands
In a grand square.
You are spoken of with reverence.

There were those three million, though,
Three million of my ancestors
Who starved on your watch.
Their bones are now ash and dust.

These things happen in war.
Some lives are expendable when bigger things are at stake.
The end result is what mattered.
Whose end, I wonder?

No one's perfect.
It is what it is.
But I am sure you will understand
If I go easy on the reverence.

Saturday bliss

It is one in the afternoon
All London is bathed in spring sunshine.
I have my car windows down
And reggae playing on the stereo.
I have done my round at the hospital
And some needless shopping too.
A book
A bunch of flowers
A bottle of wine
Custard tarts
And best of all, some early
Alphonso mangoes from the Indian shop.
If anything could exemplify bliss
This is it.
The rest of the day beckons
Even roadworks don't bother me
They let me savour the moment a bit longer.

Shot

I looked after a man who shot himself
In the foot, when out hunting one day.
His leg was amputated below the knee
He now wears a prosthesis and slowly picks his way.

Today, as unpicked daffodils wither in unmanned fields
And my builder can't fix my roof as his men are all in Poland,
I think that man with his gun is a metaphor
For an entire misguided land.

Shades of grey

It looks like we all need shades of grey in our lives.
The daily gloom against which
We can offset, fully appreciate
Bright flashes of pleasure,
Of fulfilment, or gain.
The deep bass against which
The contrapuntal riffs of joy can play.

Many of us don't have to try to do this
Life provides us with
Our daily grind
Misery in abundance.

But even those of us who are better served
Have our own pots of darkness.
To dab our minds' canvases with
We all worry.
We create
Our own shades of grey.

Neonicotinoids

What do we know of how
The last of a species dies?
Perhaps quietly by itself in a forest glade
Or deep in a burrow
Or snapped up by a predator
And we'll never know if in the end
It was starving, ill or just lonely.
Just know that we will never again
See that specific pattern on the wings
The stripes on its torso
That particular way it buzzed
Through the meadows.
You and I won't miss it
But the flowers will.

Art for two

A lifetime of seeing exhibitions and museums together
Counts for something.
If I say it's a Sisley sky you know what I mean,
Or a Magritte evening,
Or that someone has a Jamini Roy face.
At the Musée Marmottan
We talked about how the way to see a Monet
Is to scrunch up one's eyes and look at it slightly out of focus.
You correct me if I say Hiroshige to the television
In answer to the University Challenge question,
When I mean Hokusai.

BLM

So, you say you would never take a knee
And the BLM protests were dreadful.
Well, that's a view you're entitled to take.
I am sure as you said that, of your own
Privilege you were mindful.

You wouldn't rewrite history you say
But there is a certain bias
To every historical narrative.
Is it such a disaster if someone challenges
The traditional perspective?

It is time to show your true colours
It is time for you to choose
Would you rather stand with
Real people
Or would you rather protect statues?

Kintsugi

I am imperfect.
I am proud of my scars.
See them shine through
Like skeins of gold.
They make me, me.

Things to do on a wet afternoon

There's that book that is unfinished
Sitting sadly by the bedside
There's the paper you have to write
The deadline's beginning to slide.
There are things to look up on Pinterest
For home improvements pending
There are bills to pay, e-mails to answer
The task list is unending.

But no one said you have to be worthy
In deciding what to do.
Surely you can take to your sofa
Find some telly trash to view?
Open a bottle of chilled white wine
And down a glass or two,
Or better still disappear under the sheets
For a bit of baporiyu.

Baporiyu in Gujarati means making love in the afternoon.

Trolley man

There is a man I often see
Walking down the road
With all his worldly goods
In a supermarket shopping trolley.
The trolley is really full.
Bulging over with clothes
And only he knows what's
In so many plastic bags.
He struggles to push it along
As it veers this way and that.
He has to pause from time to time.
I think he needs to downsize.

Home (2)

"Where is home?" you ask
A loaded question, that!
May I pause before I answer?

Let me be literal –
Home is a red-brick semi-detached
In a modest part of London.

No, my colour isn't as light as
You might want it to be
If colour matters to you.

No, I don't like the history of empire
And I still cheer for a cricket team
That is not from these shores.

But the people here, of every hue
Are the ones I heal each day
When I go to work.

They are the ones I shall fight
Beside if this land goes to war.
This is where I live, work, pay my taxes.

These bustling city streets
This grey river
These beloved parks

This is where my ashes will be
Scattered when I die,
Where my child will continue to live.

Yes, home is a quiet, green
Corner of London.
A happy place. A journey's end.

Race relations

Your prejudice stares you in the face
You don't see it.
The knee on my brother's neck, squeezing out his breath
You don't see it.
My lot of daily indignities
You don't see it.

That I am not hitting my true potential
You don't care.
You tell me this is a land
Of equal opportunity.
You talk of aspiration in communities,
Of missing fathers and role models.
You say that it's simple, I need to lift myself
Up by my bootstraps.

You talk of nuance,
Of proportionality and appropriateness.
To you every story has
Shades of grey.
To me it is
Black and white.

Snapshots of illness

Bright sunshine, blue sky.
Magnolias in bloom.
A slight chill in the air.
A joint has been injected.
The night promises pain

* * * * * *

The fire that burned
In me has gone. I do not
Want to sail new seas.
I am content to see
My garden grow.

* * * * * *

The sky could not be bluer
Or the sun brighter
Than today.
And I am surrounded by love.
If I had to go now
I would.
Happily.

Breakfast thoughts

What part of our bodies
Do we British treasure the most?
This difficult question troubled me
As I ate my morning toast.

Naively I thought at first
Faces would come out tops
Look at how many beauty products
Are sold in all the shops.

Then I thought it may be the heart
And mine went slightly aflutter
As I proceeded to pick a second piece
And thickly spread the butter

Ah, perhaps it's the brain, I wondered
That we collectively lost
At the time of the Brexit vote,
As we now realise, to our cost.

And then suddenly the answer
Came to me in a jiffy
As I poured myself my
Second cup of coffee.

When we had a lockdown
What disappeared first from the shops?
It wasn't face cream, tampons or soap,
It wasn't baby formula, nor lamb chops.

What disappeared first, as you well know
Were packets of loo rolls
Which tells me what we value most
Are our really clean assholes.

Perspective

Just as when summer ends
You see no more swallows
If you have an expectation
Disappointment follows

Classmates

There is so much to divide us --
Distances,
Busy lives stretched for time,
Material worries,
Ill patients,
Political leanings in different directions.

And yet, when we do connect,
Be it at a gathering,
On a holiday together perhaps
Or a phone call
Or even a text message,
There is that immediate drop
Into a certain wavelength.
There is no need to pretend
Or to explain.

It was those six years together
When we went into medical school
Like lumps of pig iron
Going into the foundry
And came out as forged steel.

City morning

I have swapped my suburban existence
House, garage, garden
For a few weeks in a city flat
While builders patch up my home.

The city in summer
Still very quiet, post lockdown
Office blocks deserted
Shops limping back into business.

Walking through the canyons
You see blue sky above.
Even the trees here know
To grow vertically upwards.

Strips of sunlight
Bathe the fronts of buildings.
The smell of coffee drifts out
From the shops that have opened early.

The view from my balcony
Is of rooftops,
Distant skyscrapers —
Man-made mountains

There are no birds
To be seen or heard
Apart from the family of gulls
Nesting in a chimney across.

This morning as I awoke
I thought, surprised,
"Is that a morning chorus I hear?"
And then realised
I had been dreaming of birdsong.

Worship

My father is doing a puja.
He doesn't do this for a living
But he is descended from generations of village priests.
He knows the rituals
And will do them when the Gods
Need to be prayed to for his own family
And there isn't a priest at hand.
He is wearing his dhoti
His sacred thread is around his bare torso.
In front are the offerings to the deities --
Some flowers, chopped fruit
A copper urn and a copper spoon
To offer water to the Gods.
The little pewter and silver deities
Sit on their little throne.
Oil lamp and joss sticks.
He utters the chants clearly
And yet somewhat under his breath,
As if he does not wish to share it
With anyone else but the Gods.
I stare at him,
A wide-eyed, fascinated little boy
Not knowing then that I will never
Emulate him in this.

Charlie Parker

There's a quote by Charlie Parker
"Master your instrument,
Master the music,
And then forget all that crap
And just play".

When I operate, there is
That matter of skill
And the matter of knowledge.
Both need to there,
Embedded,
But in the background.
And I "just play".

Traffic

Traffic, endless traffic!
Infernal, soul-destroying traffic!

It makes me leave early
And still arrive late.
Resigned I am to traffic
As part of my urban fate.

My hair is turning grey by the hour,
My vision is getting blurred,
As I continue to sit in traffic
I can sense my arteries getting furred.

I could be at the pub with friends,
I could be tucked in bed with the wife.
Instead, I sit in traffic
Wasting precious hours of my life.

Every hour is rush hour
Be it dawn or dusk.
Looks like, in this giant city
Everyone always has a task

There's the school rush, the office rush,
And the hour of the articulated truck,
The white van men, the Amazon guys
And lorries carting away muck.

There are couriers zipping by on bikes
Always in such a hurry,
You might think they're delivering blood
But usually it's pizza or curry!

I can call my mom only so many times,
The chat radio is full of nutters,
Sitting in the car for hours on end
My sanity too, is in tatters.

These days, if you're going from Harrow to Harlow
Or from Dulwich over to Pinner,
You'd better wear your long-haul stockings
And take a jab of blood thinner.

Stuck in traffic on the roads and lanes
Of this infernal London town
I cannot help find myself wishing
We were all back in lockdown.

Whipple

Always beware the poem that needs an introduction! But this poem, I'm afraid, needs one. It is an invitation to get into a surgeon's head one afternoon in the operating room.

The Whipple operation is a complicated one. It is usually done to remove a tumour in the head of the pancreas. It requires anything from three to seven hours to perform and is a feat of endurance and concentration for the entire team. What is described here is a variant called the pylorus-preserving pancreatoduodenectomy. The Omni-Tract is a mechanical retractor that helps hold the wound edges apart. Not very long ago, that job used to be done by an assistant and/or a medical student. The harmonic scalpel is a dissection tool that cuts through tissues and seals the blood vessels. It makes a musical beeping noise as it does so. The stapler divides bowel and seals the cut edges with a row of fine metal staples. The thickness of stitches is described as 3/0, 4/0 etc. (spoken aloud as three-zero or three-oh). Kocher was a surgeon who described the step of the operation that involves freeing up the duodenum. The term Lahey, as used here, refers to an instrument.

If there is a deeper fulfilment than a Whipple well completed, then I haven't found it yet.

And so, knife to skin.

All uncertainties put away.
The agonising over.
Questions answered.
Tears shed.
Consent given.

The anaesthetists have worked
On her for over an hour.
The epidural's in.
She's asleep.
Tubes, lines all in place.
Central line. Arterial line.
Urine catheter. Nasogastric tube.
Monitors working.
She is on the operating table.

Checklist done.
Blood cross-matched.
Antibiotics in.
Octreotide in.
Flo-Trons on.
Lights adjusted.
All instruments present and working.

Medical students briefed.
"As you know, there are three phases
To this operation, or for that matter
To most cancer operations.
You assess.
You resect.
You reconstruct."
Scans reviewed one last time.
Fine, let's scrub.

Skin prepped and draped.
Music playing.
Glenn Gould today.
A look at the clock,
And knife to skin

A neat, straight, horizontal cut.
Not too long. Not too short.
Switch to handheld diathermy.
The smell of cauterised flesh –
My "napalm in the morning".
Buzz through the fat and the muscle.
Then peritoneum, and
The abdomen is open.

Ah, all my beautiful friends –
Nice to see you again!
Quick look and caress of the liver.
No secondaries!
Relief.

Omni-Tract time.
Clamp it on to the edge of the table.
Position the central point above the sternum
Ten centimetres above the skin.
Clamps on. Blades on.
Wound edges pulled open wide.

Quick feel of the pancreatic head
Yes, a hard lump.
Our villain du jour.
Hmm... feels mobile... good!
Quick run through the small bowel
The root of the mesentery,
All clear.
Time to start.

"Harmonic scalpel please, Sister."
Beep... beep... through the gastrocolic ligament

Stay outside of the arcade now!
Along the greater curve of the stomach.
Lesser sac open.
Beep... take down the flimsy adhesions
The veil of Larrey.
He was Napoleon's surgeon
Famous for getting a limb off swiftly
On the field of battle.
When did he find time to notice these?

So you see the body
Of the pancreas.
Salmon pink.
A bit firm to the touch,
As you would expect
With the duct blocked in the head.
Keep going to the right now.
Harmonic... beep... beep.
Free the lower aspect of the antrum and the pylorus.
Careful, tie that gastroepiploic vein
Or it will bleed!
Keep going, expose the duodenum
Free up and swing the hepatic flexure
Of the colon downwards.

Okay, gall bladder off.
Nothing wrong with it,
Just gets in the way.
Ha – it is so much easier
Taking a healthy gall bladder out!
Come on, pull the duodenum towards the left.
While I do a Kocher.
Free the duodenum along its outer edge,

Get into the plane between it and the cava.
Hmm… big fat veins.
Don't burn holes in them.
Watch that gonadal vein. And the right renal.
And the ureter.
You see the groove between cava and aorta?
A node or two there?
Take them out. Clear the fat too.
Harmonic… beep… beep
See the aorta?
Your hand now
Gets behind the entire duodenum
And you can feel the damn tumour.
Okay that's enough Kocherisation then.
Free up the third part of the duodenum a bit now.

Right, now for the hilum of the liver.
"Lahey please, Sister."
Go round and sling the bile duct
With a yellow rubber sling.
You've got to be colour-coordinated.
There's the hepatic artery
And the gastroduodenal coming off it,
Coursing down to the tumour.
Sling it.
Clip. Clip. Cut. Tie.
Suture-ligate the stump on the hepatic artery.
Don't want the bastard to bleed later.
Let's now get behind
The pancreatic neck.
Gently dissect around the lower border of the pancreatic neck
And define the SMV.
You really, really do not want

The superior mesenteric vein to bleed.
Lahey again.
Get into the plane, between the pancreas
In front, and the SMV behind.
A few millimetres at a time.
Gently, very gently.
Ah, you see the tip of the Lahey
Emerge at the top end.
"Nylon tape, Sister."
The neck of the pancreas is slung!

As we progress
The team falls into a rhythm.
Little is said.
Just hand gestures.
Just the occasional "uh-huh".
Looks over the mask.
We are in the zone.
Gradually the world
Is shut out.
All we are focused on
Is that tumour and
How it must come out.

I am Arjun.
All I see is
The eye of the fish.

By now it is obvious
That the resection is on.
Let's do the DJ flexure.
"Stapler please, Sister."
Scrunch-swoosh – the first loop of the jejunum is divided.

Harmonic again.
Beep, beep along the edge of the jejunum,
Inching towards the DJ flexure.
The ligament of Treitz comes into view.
Killed himself with cyanide, poor Treitz.
Did you know that?
Free the ligament.
Watch that IMV.
You've now got the jejunum and DJ freed.
Push it to the right
And pull it out with your left hand
Into the supracolic compartment.
Magic!

"Stapler again, Sister."
Scrunch-swoosh – the first part of the duodenum
Is divided.

Diathermy again.
Lift up that sling, boys
Let us divide the neck of the pancreas.
The diathermy smoke of each organ
Has a characteristic smell
Or so I think!
The pancreas always reminds me
Of crushed geranium petals
Or occasionally cedar wood.
As you buzz through the pancreas
– Keep it a straight vertical plane! –
A few bleeders show up
Nothing that diathermy or a stitch
Cannot sort.
Ah, there's the pancreatic duct.

A few drops of clear juice
Well out as you cut through it.
And then you have transected it completely.
Away comes the sling.
You can see the portal vein behind.
Gently lift the pancreatic stump off the splenic vein
For a centimetre or so.

Fine, bile duct next.
Snip it with scissors.
There are always two vessels that bleed
One at 3 o'clock and another at 9 o'clock.
Northover and Terblanche told us this
In 1979.
Buzz them with diathermy.
Pull out the plastic stent in the bile duct –
A manky curled length of blue plastic.
Send a bile sample for microbiology.
Tie the specimen end of the bile duct.
The other end can ooze bile for a while,
It doesn't matter.

"Sister, we will have the specimen out soon.
We'd better call Tom, the research fellow
He will want to take the specimen fresh
As soon as it comes out.
Students, can you see?
We are about to do the last bit of the dissection
But also the most hazardous bit.
Sister, have the vascular clamps handy please.
And some 4/0 Prolene sutures
Should I need them."

And so we put traction on the pancreatic head and duodenum
Pulling them to the right
And start to peel the head away
From the portal vein.
Any tiny vessels that go into the vein
Clip or suture them as they show up
You don't want them to bleed.
Gradually you have the specimen off the vein.
Behind that is the artery.
Feel it there?
Keep away from the bugger.
Again, gently pull the specimen away from the SMA
And get the little vessels as you find them.
Then suddenly,
It all comes away in your hand.
The tumour is out.

It goes into a plastic pot.
Tom shows it to the students
And then whisks it away.

We all pause.
I ask my anaesthetist,
"Is all well?
How is she doing?
Blood loss so far?
Hb? Lactate?"
So far, so good, I am told.

I turn to the team.
"Does anyone need a break?
A trip to the loo?
A cup of coffee?

Or a quick fag perhaps?"
No? All happy to carry on, it seems.
It has only been two hours.
Time flies when you are having fun.

"Students, have a look.
You won't see this anatomy often.
There's the cut end of the bile duct.
The stump of the pancreas.
You can see the pancreatic duct,
About 1 mm in diameter,
Seeping watery juice.
If allowed to leak, that seemingly innocuous
But enzyme-rich juice will play
Corrosive havoc on the tissues.
There's the cut end of the duodenum
And the cut end of the jejunum.
You can see the SMV and splenic veins join
To form the portal vein.
You can see the SMA lurking behind that.
And you can see the cava and the aorta."

Change of music?
Enough of Bach.
Can you ever have enough of Bach?
Einaudi then.
A different zone.

Let's join the bile duct first
To the bowel.
"4/0 PDS sutures please, Sister."
Interrupted. Stitches spaced one millimetre apart.
"Keep them coming."

Stitch, tie, cut. Stitch, tie, cut…
Back wall,
Then front wall.
Done!

Now, pancreas to bowel.
Every surgeon does this slightly differently.
This is the one we all worry about.
10-20% chance it may leak.
If it leaks, there may be hell to pay.

"4/0 Prolene sutures please, Sister."
Diathermy to burn a small hole in the bowel.
Single layer of sutures, four or five
To the back wall.
Full thickness of pancreas to the full thickness of the bowel.
Gentle as you snug those knots down.
Don't want the stitches to cheese-wire
Through the pancreas.
"A thin plastic infant feeding tube please, Sister.
Size? 5F or 6F should do."
Cut it to size.
Put it in as a stent into the pancreatic duct.
Front row of stitches now.
Full thickness again.
And then one additional stitch
On each side, as an extra buttress.
There, doesn't it look pretty?

Duodenum next, to be joined to jejunum.
"Slightly thicker 3/0 PDS sutures, please."
Continuous stitch for the back wall, seromuscular.
Another layer, full thickness, continuous.

Turn the corner,
Complete the run and tie it off at the end.
Another seromuscular run on the front wall?
Maybe not.
"Let's have a drain, Sister.
Place the tip of the drain behind
The bile duct."

Time to count swabs and needles.
"All good? Happy?
How many needles?
83? Hmm...
Let us close then."

Muscles with one single strong run of Prolene.
Skin with a single run of absorbable Monocryl
Just deep to the cuticle.
Looks pretty?
"All happy?"
Dressing on.
Gloves off.

Look at the clock.
Four hours? Not bad at all!
That's very good!
No transfusion? Excellent!

Write the operation notes.
Draw the diagram to explain the new plumbing.
Call her husband
From the OR itself.
"Yes, it has all gone well.
Yes, but this is just the first step.

Yes, you can see her in the critical care unit
Maybe a couple of hours from now."

Make sure the Octreotide is written up,
As is the Tinzaparin.
No need for more antibiotic.
"Yes, she can sip when she is awake.
The nasogastric tube can come out
Tomorrow.
You've got the procedure code?"
Quick debrief. It all went well.
"Thank you, Sister.
Thank you team.
Bye for now."

As I walk out of the OR
Towards that cup of coffee,
I check my cell phone –
There are seven messages.
The afternoon has passed.
It is dark.
My neck hurts.

NOTES

Thank you for coming this far with me. Here are some explanatory notes:

Mare Nostrum
This was the Roman name for the Mediterranean Sea. Operation Mare Nostrum was an operation run by the Italian government over 2013-14 to bring migrants adrift in the sea, to Europe.

23rd June 2016
If you are wondering about the date, it was the day the United Kingdom voted on Brexit.

The sun always rises in Akola
VT was Victoria Terminus, now known by a different name.

Kihim afternoon
Kihim is a beach near Alibag, not far from Mumbai.

Vincent
Written after a day at the Van Gogh Museum in Amsterdam.

End of CPR
CPR stands for cardiopulmonary resuscitation.

September 2020
I am in debt to W B Yeats and his poem 'September 1913'.

A song for the NHS
The NHS is the National Health Service.
A P45 is the salary and tax notice you receive when you leave an employment.

Popat
Popat is the Marathi word for a parakeet.

The OR is of course the operating room.

Printed in Great Britain
by Amazon